Plants need
CARBON

Our farm

Here is our farm.

Look at the sugar cane.

We **grow** sugar cane

on our farm.

Water and sun

Look at the water.

The sugar cane needs

the water to grow.

water

Here is the sun.

The sugar cane needs

the sun to grow.

8

sun

Carbon

The sugar cane needs carbon to grow.

Carbon is in the leaves.

Carbon is in the roots.

leaves

roots

11

Where is the carbon?

Look at the leaves.

Can you see the holes?

The carbon goes in the holes.

The carbon is in the plant.

holes

Plants need carbon to grow.

Glossary

grow

plants